Evexiandros

"The Wellness Seeker"

Southeast Asia

Ancient and Traditional Healing Secrets

Copyright:

Table of Contents:

About the Author:

My name is Mano. I'm an author, blogger, and documentary filmmaker, but besides that, I'm a Natural medicine researcher. My real passion is the search for wellness. I travel around the world and I explore traditional medicine secrets, alternative treatments, folk healing practices, superfoods, physical activities for well-being, meditation techniques, and philosophy pathways. I'm seeking healing in every corner of this planet. My real name is Emmanuil, but my author's pen name is **Evexiandros**. I change it, as according to the Ancient Greeks, names should be created by the way you lived your life. Evexiandros in Greek means Men of Wellness, much like my website: (www.thewellnessseeker.com).

Our Products are Strictly for Wellness Collectors:

Ancient and Traditional Healing Secrets Series:

This book series is a wellness world encyclopedia and is dedicated to all kinds of travelers, healers, mystics, and natural medicine lovers. The wellness seeker (Evexiandros) discovers ancient traditional healing secrets and seeks medical treatments in the most remote regions of the globe. Rediscover ancient healing practices before they get lost in history.

Traditional Medicine, Alternative Treatments, Spirituality, Folk Healing Practices, Superfoods, Herbal Medicine, Spa Therapies, Physical Activities for Well-being, Meditation, Philosophy Pathways.

Just think about it... What's the main reason you travel? Whether you're on stunning white sand beaches or climbing imposing mountains. Whether you're enjoying exotic cuisines or exploring ancient temples, it's all just a state of physical and spiritual well-being. Use these travel guidebooks in order to improve your health and well-being.

Introduction:

Ancient and Traditional Healing Secrets
Southeast Asia:

Southeast Asia is a place of extreme beauty and wilderness. The Spiritual practices and philosophies of Hinduism and Theravada Buddhism have influenced the food, martial arts, and way of living. Mindfulness, meditation, self-awareness, and compassion are some of the practices that travelers learn in Southeast Asia. I have visited almost all Southeast Asia countries: Thailand, Singapore, Laos, Indonesia, Philippines, Vietnam, Malaysia, Myanmar, and Cambodia. Are you looking for wellness in Southeast Asia?

Learn traditional dances, visit the nicest beaches, find the best massage treatments, and practice martial arts for your well-being. For sure is one of the best destinations to visit for wellness and natural therapies. Herbs and Medicinal parts of the plants are used by many ethnic groups in Southeast Asia. As I lived, in Southeast Asia for more than 15 years, this is not just a book is a life journey.

Southeast Asia Health Tips and Guidelines:

Here are some general health recommendations for certain Southeast Asian nations that I have visited.

Thailand Health Travel Tips:

Thailand Healthcare System:

Thailand's healthcare system is excellent. Thailand has a large number of English-speaking general practitioners, dentists, and opticians. Most large provinces have at least one private hospital, with many more in prominent tourist locations.

Vaccinations for Thailand:

While no immunizations are advised for Thailand, you may want to consider the following:

MMR, Polio, Diptheria, and Tetanus immunizations are all recommended.

Rabies is a disease that affects humans. The risk to travelers is low, the rabies vaccination is worth considering if you plan to be in remote locations.

Hepatitis A is a virus that causes liver disease.

Hepatitis B is a virus that causes liver disease.

Typhoid fever is a disease that affects people. It's good to have this vaccine if you are planning to spend a considerable amount of your trip in rural locations.

Tap Water:
Only drink boiling or treated water in Thailand, never tap water.

Air quality:
Air pollution can be severe in major cities, like Bangkok and Chiang Mai, which are also affected by the regional smoke haze. High levels of pollution and PM 2.5 occasionally reach unsafe and dangerous levels.

Diseases in Thailand:
Because Thailand is located in the tropics, its climate is hot, and when combined with humidity or monsoonal rains, it creates an ideal setting for diseases and other health dangers to thrive, such as Malaria and Dengue Fever.

Emergency Treatment:
Call 1669 for immediate nationwide emergency assistance.

Is Street Food Safe in Thailand?
While traveling in Thailand, you'll come across a wide range of tasty food, but is it safe to eat? Don't eat anything that's been sitting around for a while, even if it's only been a few minutes. It's better if it's fresh. Choose food vendors with a large crowd, locals will quickly figure out which ones are safe. Keep an eye out for stalls that appear to be clean.

Bali Health Travel Tips:

Bali has long been renowned as one of the best tourist destinations for well-being. It's a beautiful island that is in harmony with nature, With beautiful beaches, lush forests, natural hot springs, and friendly people. The predominantly Hindu Island has strong spiritual roots and amazing energies.

Emergency Treatment:
For emergency medical treatment the phone number to dial is 911.

Tap Water:
It is in general safe to drink tap water in Bali.

Vaccinations:
In general, travelers don't need vaccinations for Bali, except the yellow fever vaccination. Your doctor may also recommend, Tetanus Single booster, Typhoid, Hepatitis A, and Rabies vaccinations.

Bali Health Care System and Hospitals:
Bali Health Care System, may not be the best in the world but can be trusted, as is one of the best in Indonesia. The main public hospitals of the island are located in Denpasar. Bali Health Care has it all from small clinics to all-encompassing hospitals. Unfortunately, private hospitals are expensive that's why most ex-pats in Bali go to medical clinics.

Laos Health Travel Tips:

Healthcare in Laos:

Laos' poverty rate has dropped from 40% to 23%, while the average life expectancy has improved from 57 to 67 years, according to the World Health Organization (WHO). Although there have been major developments in the country, Laos' healthcare system is still in its infancy. Medical treatment in Laos remains insufficient and unequally distributed due to flaws in the financing, health records, infrastructure, and management of health services.

Emergency Treatment:

For emergency medical treatment the phone number to dial is 1195.

Tap Water:

It is not recommended to drink the water from the tap in Laos. Water supplies in Laos are harmed by a variety of factors, including human waste, chemical pollution, aging water pipes, and water treatment facilities.

Vaccinations:

In Laos, various immunizations are recommended or necessary. Hepatitis A, B, typhoid, cholera, yellow fever, Japanese encephalitis, rabies, meningitis, polio, measles, mumps, and rubella (MMR), diphtheria, tetanus, and pertussis, shingles, chickenpox, pneumonia, and influenza are among the vaccines recommended by the CDC and WHO for Laos.

Cambodia Health Travel Tips:

Healthcare in Cambodia:
While there are some well-regarded hospitals and clinics in and around Phnom Penh, medical facilities in more remote locations are few and far between. In addition to these challenges, significant medical consequences are frequently not treated in Cambodia, necessitating treatment abroad. As a result, whether you plan to travel to Cambodia or migrate as an expat, you must have a thorough understanding of the Cambodian healthcare system.

Emergency Treatment:
For emergency medical treatment the phone number to dial is 119.

Tap Water:
It is generally not advised to drink tap water in Cambodia.

Vaccinations:
The following vaccines are indicated in a variety of situations, but each case must be evaluated individually. Previous immunizations or allergies, your health history, and other lifestyle concerns are all important. Hepatitis A, Hepatitis B, Typhoid, Malaria, Japanese Encephalitis, and Rabies.

Singapore Health Travel Tips:

Healthcare in Singapore:
Singapore has a world-class healthcare system that the USA administration's healthcare team is studying as a model as it looks for ways to modernize the US healthcare system. The World Health Organization (WHO) classified Singapore's healthcare system as the finest in Asia in 2000, ahead of Hong Kong and Japan.

Emergency Treatment:
For emergency medical treatment the phone number to dial is 995.

Tap Water:
In Singapore, you can drink the tap water. Singapore is one of the few countries where the tap water is safe to drink.

Vaccinations:
While no immunizations are advised for Singapore all travelers should have their normal vaccines up to date, according to the Centers for Disease Control and Prevention (CDC).

Malaysia Health Travel Tips:

Healthcare in Malaysia:
All citizens and legal residents in Malaysia have access to universal healthcare. Malaysia has a two-tier healthcare system: government-run universal healthcare and a private healthcare system that coexists. Expats can go to whichever hospital they want, and if they don't have insurance, they can pay out of pocket.

Emergency Treatment:
For emergency medical treatment the phone number to dial is 999.

Tap Water:
In Malaysia, tap water is not safe to drink. Although the tap water in Kuala Lumpur is extensively chlorinated and hence safe, the pipes that transport it may not be.

Vaccinations:
While no immunizations are advised for Malaysia all travelers should have their normal vaccines up to date, according to the Centers for Disease Control and Prevention (CDC).

Vietnam Health Travel Tips:

Healthcare in Vietnam:
Travelers going to Vietnam will find a healthcare system that treats most medical conditions by combining components of Eastern and Western treatment. Currently, most Vietnamese individuals must pay for their own medical care in both public and private facilities. People who can afford it often choose to use private facilities since they are better equipped and more efficient.

Emergency Treatment:
For emergency medical treatment the phone number to dial is 115.

Tap Water:
In Vietnam, it is typically not recommended to drink tap water. Water polluted with harmful organisms is a major source of illness, including diarrhea, gastroenteritis, typhoid, cholera, and dysentery.

Vaccinations:
Although no immunizations are required by law for visitors to enter Vietnam, several vaccinations are widely advised. Hepatitis A, B, typhoid, Japanese encephalitis, rabies, meningitis, polio, measles, mumps, and rubella (MMR), tetanus, diphtheria, and pertussis, chickenpox, shingles, pneumonia, and influenza are among the vaccines recommended by the CDC and WHO for Vietnam.

Myanmar Health Travel Tips:

Healthcare in Myanmar:
Myanmar's (commonly known as Burma) healthcare system is poor. From 1962 through 2011, the military administration spent 0.5 percent to 3% of the country's GDP on healthcare. Myanmar's healthcare is frequently listed among the world's worst.

Emergency Treatment:
For emergency medical treatment the phone number to dial is 192.

Tap Water:
In Myanmar, tap water is unsafe to drink. Bottled water is readily accessible throughout the country.

Vaccinations:
Although no vaccinations are officially required to enter Myanmar, a variety of immunizations are suggested or required like the yellow fever vaccination.

Philippines Health Travel Tips:

Healthcare in Philippines:
The good news is that English is widely spoken in the Philippines, which is a huge plus. Medical personnel in the Philippines are well-trained, although facilities may not be as remarkable as those in high-end US or European institutions. The quality of public healthcare in the Philippines differs greatly between rural and metropolitan locations. In the Philippines, private healthcare is far more consistent, and facilities are generally better equipped than public ones.

Emergency Treatment:
For emergency medical treatment the phone number to dial is 911.

Tap Water:
Because to their lack of infrastructure, it is not recommended to drink tap water in the Philippines.

Vaccinations:
Although no vaccinations are officially required to enter Philippines, a variety of immunizations are suggested or required like the yellow fever vaccination.

My First Experiences in Southeast Asia:

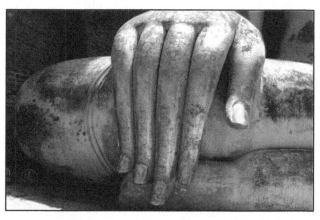

Southeast Asia is composed of eleven countries that extend from eastern India to China and is divided into two zones: mainland and island. Southeast Asia, sometimes called Indochina, is a conglomeration of linked but disparate countries wedged between the Indian and Pacific Oceans. The area has long been a popular destination for globe-trotting backpackers, thanks to its gorgeous beaches, delectable cuisine, kind and welcoming people, inexpensive pricing, and convenient air connections. The first country that I visited in Southeast Asia in 1998 was Thailand. I went to Phuket and Bangkok and I fell in love with the culture and way of living. I was 24 years old and I had already traveled to most places in Europe. As a big fan of the lonely planet travel guides, In the year 2000, I bought my first digital video camera with the intention of creating a website and sharing my adventures with the rest of the world. This idea seemed insane at the time.

My website did well, so I spent the summers working in Greece during the tourist high season and in the winter, I was traveling around Asia and made travel films, which I was selling on my website. Thailand was my base, and from there I traveled around Asia but mostly Southeast Asia. Nine years later, I opened a restaurant in Thailand which I'll explain more about it later, and managed for ten years until Covid change the world as we know it

Nutrition in Southeast Asia:

Nutrition in Southeast Asia is a very important subject. Southeast Asian cuisines are richer in flavor and worldwide famous for their healthy ingredients. With dozens of health-boosting herbs, vegetables, and spices the food in Southeast Asia is a delicious experience and every dish offers a journey to the culture and history. Like in any other place in Asia, rice is the main food. During my travels in Southeast Asia, I had the opportunity to taste some of the most popular dishes.

Malaysia and Singapore Cuisines:

Chinese and Indian cultures have a strong influence on Malaysian cuisine. There are so many delicious Malaysian dishes to try, and for sure Nasi lemak is one of them. In Petaling Street, I tried the Malay Nasi Lemak with Fried Chicken for the first time. Nasi lemak means fat rice and is the national and traditional dish of Malaysia. It's spicy coconut rice, traditionally served with anchovy hot chili sauce, anchovies, cucumbers, peanuts, and boiled eggs. In Singapore and Kuala Lumpur China towns, you will find authentic Chinese food. Traditional Chinese-style peanut pancake is a common street-snack in Southeast Asia countries. Chinese peanut pancake has peanut filling sandwiched in between and contains red bean paste or cream corn. Like Malaysia, Singapore is an absolute paradise for food lovers. Traditional Chinese cuisine is everywhere in Singapore. Chinese cuisine was brought to Singapore by Chinese immigrants in the 19th century. Many of the dishes have evolved and mixed with ingredients found in Southeast Asia. The Chinese way of eating is healthy and extends the lifespan, filled with protein and fiber-rich vegetables.

Myanmar Cuisine:

During my visit to Myanmar, I explored the exotic tastes of Burmese cuisine which in my opinion, it has similarities and influences to Thai, Chinese and Indian cuisines. I enjoy eating in restaurants but also at street food stands. Although Burmese cuisine has not much variety it holds some really healthy ingredients. Burmese Curry is the most common food in Myanmar. Especially the Burmese Chicken Curry.

It is made with turmeric, coconut milk, garam masala, ginger, lemongrass, and fish sauce. Another must-try dish in Myanmar is Mohinga. Mohinga, it's a hot-sour fish soup served with noodles and is the national dish of Myanmar. This traditional soup has some of my favorite healthy Southeast Asian ingredients: Lemongrass, ginger, turmeric, fish sauce, galangal, and tamarind.

Indonesian Cuisine:

Ubud village it's for sure the best place that I have visited in Bali. Ubud means medicine and as a medicinal village, it becomes a magnet for healers, yogis, and natural health

practitioners. Indonesian cuisine is based on fresh spices and colorful healthy herbs. The best place to have your food as medicine is Ubud. Having dinner in a traditional place like Ubud Village allows you to enjoy the Balinese culture and food at the same time. Balinese people are passionate about their spices, and one of the best ways to taste the Indonesian herbs and spices is by trying

NASI GORENG. Nasi Goreng is the national dish of Indonesia and means fried rice. It is actually the Indonesian version of fried rice.

Vietnamese Cuisine:

Hanoi is located on the banks of the Red River. Together with Ho Chi Minh the Vietnamese capital of Hanoi provides some of the best restaurants and Street Food experiences. It is a great place to explore the local cuisine as many of the popular Vietnamese dishes originated here. Vietnamese food  has become very popular around the world in the past few years. Vietnamese cuisine was influenced by the French colonial empire and its nearby neighbors. China, Laos, Cambodia, and Thailand. Banh mi is the Vietnamese national sandwich and the word for bread. This bread is a legacy of the France colony. Compared to the France baguettes, the Vietnamese-style baguettes are lighter, thinner, and crispier. In Vietnamese markets, food explorers will find all kinds of goods. Vietnamese people love noodles. Pho is a famous noodle soup with beef and beef bones or chicken that simmered for hours before being served and made with various aromatic herbs and spices like ginger, cardamom pods, star anise, cloves, and cinnamon.

Thai Cuisine:

As I lived in Pattaya Thailand for many years and opened a small food stall that later became a Mediterranean restaurant. I have a lot of experience with Thai cooking. I opened in 2009 as a street food stall with a few tables and served Greek food such as Souvlaki, Dolmadakia, Moussaka, and many other traditional Greek dishes. I have a lot of beautiful memories of this little food stall and I made a lot of friends. After four years that I was there, the owner, unfortunately, sold the land and we had to change location. As things were going well with this business, that allowed me to grow and make it a small Mediterranean

restaurant. I kept this restaurant for ten years. In my restaurant, I had healthy Mediterranean dishes and some Asian plates (mostly Thai).

Is Thai Food Healthy?

Thai food is fresh and delicious. Many Thai dishes are steamed or stir-fried which is good for your health. Spices used in Thai cuisine like galangal root, turmeric, lemongrass, ginger, and chilies are all immune system boosters. Another great thing about Thai food is that normally, Thais will have a plate of assorted fresh raw herbs and vegetables near their main dish. Thai dishes like Tom Yum Soup have been under scientific study for their incredible health benefits. Finally, Thais cook fast. Quick-cooking allows food to retain its natural, essential vitamins and minerals.

In general, Traditional Thai food consider healthy, as they use all-natural and fresh ingredients, but what about today? Thai food can be deceiving. Many people coming to Thailand think that have found the best way to lose kilos without consequences. But what they don't know is how much sugar, sodium, palm oil, and MSGs (Monosodium glutamate) Thai people use when cooking. Palm oil can be threatening to your health, as is very high in saturated fat. Saturated fats, increased cholesterol levels, can be really bad for your heart. Sugar is the worst ingredient in the modern diet. MSG has been used as a food additive for decades. A flavor enhancer that's known widely as an addition, to Asian food. MSG comes in many processed foods and snacks. Some people called it the silent killer, as it is worse health slowly. But apart from all that, another danger of Thai food is that Thai people don't use freezers. Especially if you eat Thai food from street stalls or cheaper restaurants. They leave meat and eggs out all day and as a result, bacteria take over. Even if bacteria die after cooking long, toxins can remain if the food was out for so long.

Conclusion:

Homemade Thai food is one of the best for your health. If you can't cook at home, at least know if your Thai restaurant uses unhealthy ingredients! Ask them if they use Palm-oil, MSGs, or any other thing that is bad for your health.

Eating Insects in Thailand:

Eating insects is a very common practice in Thailand. It actually originated in Northeastern places like Isan. Over 50 species of bugs are edible. Bamboo worms, silkworm pupae, water beetles, Grasshoppers, Scorpions, locusts, crickets, red ants, and so on. I tried once ant eggs and Grasshoppers. Not my favorite food, but Edible insects contain a high-quality protein similar to beef. In Thailand's markets, you'll find bins brimming with delectable insects. Bamboo worms are popular among Thais because they have a corn-like flavor and are slightly fibrous. Chili and lemongrass are used in the preparation of the insects, which are served over rice.

Top Healthy Thai Dishes:

Thailand has one of the most popular cuisines worldwide, blending elements of several southeastern Asian traditions. I prefer dishes without meat, but on meat-days, I enjoy some of these delicious dishes. The spiciness of Thai cuisine is well known. Many Thai dishes can be ordered with chicken (gai) or pork (moo) interchanged as well as with all kinds of vegetable (Pak) variations. Here is a list of the top Thai dishes to try if you're visiting Thailand or a Thai restaurant.

Bami Mu Daeng (Noodle Soup with Grilled Pork):
Often served with chilies in vinegar, and dried chili flakes.

Pla Neung Manao (Steamed Fish with Lime Dressings):
A steamed whole fish with lime dressing. It's one of Thailand's most requested fish dishes and served over a portable furnace of smoking embers in a fish-shaped metal dish.

Moo Pad Prik Khing (pork stir-fried with chili paste):
Pad Prik Khing is a simple dish with meat and green beans mixed with chili paste, red pepper, garlic and kaffir lime leaves.

Pad Ka Pow (Spicy Basil Stir Fry):
A very traditional Thai breakfast and is usually served with a fried egg. Pad Krapow is a ubiquitous fast-food dish in Thailand. It is a definite staple in the Thai diet and one of my favorites.

Gai Pad Khing (Ginger Chicken):
The classic chicken with Ginger, is a simple Thai stir-fry of sliced chicken, ginger, mushrooms, garlic, and onions.

Tom Yum:
One of the key meals that characterizes Thai flavor is Tom Yum, which is both hot and sour. It's one of the most popular dishes among Thais and tourists alike. The original Tom Yum soup does not contain coconut milk.

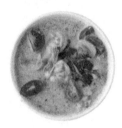

Tom Yum Goong, in my opinion, is an excellent cold and flu medicine. It consists of soup stock with herbs like lemongrass, galangal, kaffir lime leaf, and a choice of meat or seafood.

Pad Preow Wan khai (Thai Sweet and Sour Chicken):
A sweet and sour dish. This sweet and sour chicken is a mouth-watering stir fry dish with tomatoes, onions, pineapple, spring onion, cucumber, and mixed capsicum.

Khao Pad (Fried Rice):

It's a very easy and fast dish to make and is considered one of the best fast-food dishes in Thailand. It's made with meat, seafood, or just vegetables.

Pad Thai Moo or Gai:

It is a wonderful combination of noodles, chicken or pork, crunchy fresh veggies and that distinctive sweet and tangy sauce.

Panang:

Panang curry paste is traditionally made from chili peppers and coconut milk. Thai Panang curry is one of the most popular curries among westerners and Thais.

Som Tam (Thai papaya salad):

Som tam is one of the spiciest dishes available. After you try it, you'll understand why this green papaya salad is so popular around the world.

Tom Jued Soup (Thai Clear Soup with Minced Pork):

This clear Soup with Minced Pork it's super delicious. Unlike tom yum, which is usually heavy on spice and citrus, Tom Jued Soup is clear.

Yam Talay Salad (Seafood Salad):

This lovely salad will be a great addition to your lunch.

Khao Man Gai:

Hainanese chicken rice is a dish that is incredibly famous throughout Southeast Asia. Khao man gai is the Thai version of this dish.

Filipino Cuisine:

Filipino food is influenced by Spanish cooking and includes elements of Mexican food as well as American fast-food. I tried once Tuslob-Buwa, a cooked pig's brain with the liver.

Food in the Philippines is Bad:

The population of the Philippines is growing rapidly, with 108.12 million people in the latest years. According to the World Health Organization and a study, obesity has a strong impact in the Philippines due to a large number of obese persons in the country. The report said that more than 18 million Filipinos are overweight. The Philippines and especially Manila is the Mecca of fast junk food. This is my third trip to the Philippines, and I can assure you that things have worsened since my previous visits. Even the so-called healthy choices on stalls with fruit juices and detox fruit teas are most of the time full of sugar. Without a doubt, Filipinos don't know how to cook and don't have any food culture. But I don't blame them alone for that. Filipinos, unfortunately, are victims of America's junk epidemic. Besides that, even brands like McDonald's or Burger king taste worse here, as all of this fried food is cooked with bad palm oil and poor ingredients. Seriously, the food does not only taste bad, but it is also very dangerous for your stomach, especially if you have Irritable Bowel Syndrome, GERD, or Gastritis. Even when we tried Japanese restaurants as a better option the food was fatty and oily. This is why Filipino food is considered one of the worse foods in Asia. It is so hard to find something green in Manila, salads are rare here or ridiculously expensive. Jollibee is a Filipino multinational chain of fast-food restaurants and is the first choice of Filipino young people. That's just a disappointment as the Philippines is a beautiful country.

Southeast Asia Organic Farming Bio Products:

L ike any other place in the world today, Southeast Asia has a major interest in organic products. Southeast Asia Organic farming and bio-products have grown in recent years. Organic foods have exploded in popularity since 2000. The reason behind this is that organic food is grown without the use of human-made synthetic chemicals and does not contain genetically modified organisms (GMOs).

Thailand:

Thailand is an agricultural country and can produce the best quality bio-organic products. Permaculture Institute of Thailand promotes organic farming to encourage sustainable agriculture. You can find Organic products on almost every corner. Especially in Bangkok, Pattaya, and Chiang Mai. Nonprofit Organizations like the Thai Organic Farming Development Foundation help Thai farmers break the poverty cycle and convert to organic farming.

BIO - Organic Product Stores:

Spana is one of the best services for Spa. With 17years in the spa business, Spana has high-quality essential massage oils, body creams, body and foot scrubs, and in general all spa accessories.

Herb Basics in Chiang Mai is also a good place to buy organic high-quality herbal extracts and aromatherapy products. Located in The Nimman hemit road next to Think Park. Chang Noi Herb is a good choice for herbal products like coconut oil and herbal Toiletries.

Laos:

Lao people are very energetic. Cardiovascular conditioning exercises are very popular all across Southeast Asia. In Vientiane, you will see groups exercising every morning and evening on the boardwalk and park along the Mekong River. In general, Lao people try to stay healthy so you will find a lot of organic farming agricultural products and fresh food.

Vientiane had a lot of nice surprises and as a big fan of natural products, I had to visit the renowned T'Shop Lai Gallery.

The place opened in 1997 and has a lot of natural products like organic soaps, lip balms, herbal teas, and fragrant candles. All made by "Les Artisan Lao" a brand selling and producing natural products.

Philippines:

I have visited the Philippines 3 times already and within those years many changes have happened, fortunately, this time for something good. The Philippines ranked fifth on the list of countries with the largest number of organic producers. With nearly 150,000 hectares, the Philippines have the largest organic coconut area. Davao Region is the top coconut producer, contributing 14.4% to the country's total production. Herbal supplements are derived from plants, roots, berries, seeds, and flowers, and are used for their healing properties. Although it may be difficult to find healthy food in the Philippines, there are plenty of natural bio-organic products available in Filipino shopping malls, especially in Manila and Angeles City. Carica Herbal Health Products is a good choice for functional foods and food supplements. With over 30 stores in the Philippines, Healthy Options is the first and largest all-natural organic products retailer since 1995.

Southeast Asian Superfoods and Medicinal Plants:

O n my journeys to Southeast Asia, I discover many Medicinal Plants, Herbs, and Superfoods. People place a high value on a healthy ecosystem and wildlife. Animals have a special bonding with human beings and different wild animals have different benefits to the human race. Southeast Asian tribes are connected to nature. The knowledge of some medicinal plants is obtained by observing the behavior of animals. The national symbol of Thailand, the elephants are admired for their strength, endurance, and plant-based diet. Animals will modify their diet and seek medicinal herbs, flowers, or plants when they are feeling sick. Even butterflies are self-medicating with plants. Some animals like monkeys apply substances with medicinal properties to their skin. Monkeys have special repellents for insects like citrus juices. Chimpanzees eat a piece of bark to treat gastrointestinal disorders. Many Lizards species eat a particular anti-venom root when bit by a venomous snake. Snakebite has been a major cause of mortality across tropical countries. Anti-snake plants and roots, from ethnomedicine reports, are studied for many years.

Zoopharmacognosy and Tribal Medicine:

With Zoopharmacognosy, many exotic plant species were used to treat health conditions by local healers. In Lao, the Hmong ethnic group has extensive knowledge about the use of medicinal plants. Herbs and Medicinal parts of the plants are used by many ethnic groups in Southeast Asia. Acquisition of this knowledge has a long history. Thailand has many tribes that use traditional medicinal plants.

Traditional healers still play an important role in local health care systems. Padaung the hill tribe that women wear rings on the neck is not individual, but they belong to a group of Karen.

The Karen hill-tribe, guard substantial ethnomedicinal plant knowledge, as documented in many studies. The gold triangle is called like this because here is the biggest plantation of opium in the world. Here they live the forgotten nomadic tribe of Akha.

The Burmese tribe of Akha is one of the six major tribes or minorities living in the remote hills of northern Thailand who still use extensively plants as medicines. Galangal, Lemongrass, Butterfly Pea, Betelnut, Krachai dam, Butea Superba, Bean sprouts, Tongkat Ali, Chameleon plant are some of the many Southeast Asian medicinal plants and herbs used by tribal groups. Here is a full list of the most important Southeast Asian superfoods and medicinal plants.

Butterfly Pea:
It's known for its gorgeous colors. Butterfly Pea flower is another amazing herb that I found here in Thailand. That herb was mentioned on a website for asthma treatments, and I discovered it in person during a trip to Chiang Mai.

Let's study the usage and health advantages of butterfly pea. As a tea, it is normally mixed with dried lemongrass and is full of potent antioxidants. Butterfly Pea (Clitoria ternatea) is also used in Chinese and Ayurvedic medicine. Here are some health benefits of this plant:

Antioxidant Properties: Like green tea, butterfly pea flower tea is full of potent antioxidants.

Analgesic Properties: Butterfly pea tea is proven to have analgesic properties.

Anti-inflammatory Properties: This tea helps you to reduce inflammation in the body.

Good for your Brain: Contains Acetylcholine, which can increase the levels of Acetylcholine in the brain.

Anti-cancer Properties: That tea has anti-cancer properties, it penetrates the cancer cell membranes and inhibits their growth.

Conjunctivitis Treatment: In Thailand, butterfly pea is used to treat eye infections like 'red-pink eye infection'

It Prevents Allergies: This flowering herb is also rich in flavonoids. In humans, flavonoids provide numerous protective health benefits.

It Helps Strengthen Weak Hair: Butterfly Pea sometimes comes as an ingredient in shampoos and conditioners, as can reduce greying of hair and promote hair growth.

Improve Skin: It's good for your skin as it helps lessen wrinkles and rejuvenate the skin.

Anti-depressant Properties: In a study, Butterfly-pea tea was able to reduce the biological impact of stress on rats. So yes this tea can reduce stress in Humans.

Anti-Asthmatic: This herb is very good for the common cold, cough & asthma and helps to clear mucus and sputum production in respiratory organs.

Sugarcane:
In Ayurvedic medicine is believed that sugarcane juice is an excellent liver detox. As it is an energy booster juice, it's rich in carbohydrates, protein, iron, and potassium. Sugarcane juice is diuretic and can treat urinary tract infections and kidney stones.

Galangal:
The most important health benefit of galangal root is that acts as an anti-cancer agent. According to studies, galangal extracts showed antidiabetic, antimicrobial, anti-inflammatory, and analgesic properties. *Black Galangal* is used in Thai traditional medicine as a natural testosterone booster for

erectile dysfunction in males and as a sex drive herb in females. Krachai Dum is famous in many countries of Southeast Asia as a natural Viagra.

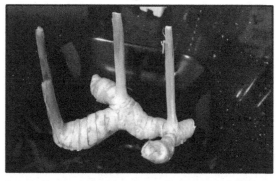

It contains substantial amounts of PDE5 inhibitors, which act like Viagra, but without the negative side effects. It is one of the best herbs for erectile dysfunction. Krachai in the Thai language means Kaempferia-Galanga. So, the real translation for this Thai root (Krachaidam) in English is Black Galangal and not Black Ginger! It is an herbaceous plant belonging to the Zingiberaceae family (Ginger family). Some say that after Horny Goat Weed, Black Galangal is the most powerful PDE5 inhibitor and research has backed up these claims. Krachaidam or Black Ginger is available in the market in various product forms. I used it with zinc for better results. This root will help you a lot with libido, but do not expect the same effects as a Viagra. Krachai Dum is well-known for a variety of other health benefits. Thai doctors are using black ginger for the prevention of strokes. This root has also anti-plasmodial, anti-inflammatory, anti-allergic, antioxidant, anti-fungal, anti-mycobacterial, and adaptogenic activity. Aside from improving erectile function, studies have shown that it increases sperm density. According to other research, it increases physical fitness performance and muscular endurance.

It stops psoriasis flares. It lowers blood glucose levels and improves blood flow. It reduces triglycerides and helps with gastric ulcers. Finally, it is used as a natural antidepressant. Black Galangal doses to increase libido: Drink twice a day 30 mg of Black Ginger liqueur (without alcohol). Better when you wake up and before you go to bed.

Tongkat Ali.

I saw Tongkat-Ali (Eurycoma Longifolia) for the first time in Thailand. It is native to Malaysia, Burma, Thailand, and Indonesia. This medicinal plant has been shown in studies to increase testosterone and libido in men.

Lemongrass:

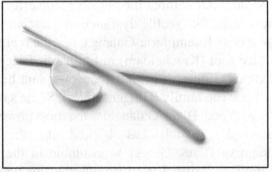

Lemongrass is a popular herb in Southeast Asian cooking. Many studies have shown the health and medicinal benefits of this plant. Lemongrass is high in antioxidants and has anti-hyperlipidemic, anti-microbial, and anti-bacterial properties. It detoxifies the body, it is beneficial in reducing inflammation in gastrointestinal disorders. Relieves insomnia, reduces fever, reduces aches, and helps with boosting metabolism.

Bitter Melon:

Normally, it grows in tropical areas. Bitter melon or Goya fruit is safe for most people and is commonly used for beneficial health reasons. Many bitter foods are promoted for their health benefits, and this melon is no exception. The fruit and seeds are used to make medicine. Bitter melon is also known as bitter gourd, Karela, Goya, Balsam Pear, or simply Bitter Squash in English. Though Goya's taste is very bitter, inside is full of beneficial antioxidants and vitamins. The healing properties of Bitter Melon are becoming more and more accepted worldwide.

Tamarind:

There are two main types of tamarind, the sweet, which comes from Thailand, and the sour. It is an amazing fruit with many health benefits. This fruit has anti-inflammatory and antibacterial effects and is one of the best for the detoxification of the liver. Tamarind lowers the bad cholesterol (LDL) and increases the good (HDL). It fights inflammation and may relieve stomach aches and constipation.

Dokudami:

Dokudami is mostly known as a panacea in Vietnam, China, Thailand, Laos, Cambodia, Japan, India, and Korea. While living in Asia, one of the things I enjoyed was researching new medicinal plants that are not known in Europe. I saw Chameleon Plant for the first time in Thailand. Plukaw is the Thai name for it. The chameleon plant is also known as a Chinese lizard tail or Houttuynia cordata. It belongs to the Saururaceae family. In southeast Asia, is traditionally used to cure various human diseases. In India, they use the plant externally, to treat snake bites and skin disorders. Chinese used a Chameleon Plant injection since ancient times and it has proved to relieve symptoms of pneumonia and asthma. Dokudami Properties: A chameleon plant has many activities and properties: Anti-mutagenic, anti-aging, anti-cancer, anti-diabetic, anti-allergic, anti-leukemic, anti-bacterial, anti-inflammatory, anti-obesity, hepatoprotective, anti-viral, and anti-microbial. It is also rich in Potassium, Magnesium, Calcium, and Sodium. *Dokudami side effects*: Are not any known side effects for this plant. A recent Chinese study found that injection form may cause severe allergic reactions in some people.

Young Ginger:

(King On) is picked earlier than ginger and has a more subtle flavor. The skin can be left on for cooking.

Bean Sprout "Thua Ngok":

These sprouts give you an easy way to boost the nutrients in your diet. Bean sprouts have the richest source of amino acids and contain all types of vitamins A, B, C, D, E and K, iron, potassium, calcium, magnesium and zinc.

41

Cassava Root "Sam Pa Lang":
Cassava is very similar to potatoes but has nearly twice the calories of potatoes. It can be boiled, steamed, baked, grilled, fried, or mashed. High in Fiber, magnesium, copper vitamin C, and folate.

Lotus Root: "Raug Bua":
It is actually the rhizome of the lotus plant. Rich in vitamin C and B-6, Fiber, potassium, magnesium and calcium.

Taro Root: "Puak":
Taro is the root of the taro plant. It lowers your blood sugar levels, protects the skin, boosts vision, prevents heart disease, and increases circulation.

Betel Nut:
Betel nut is popular in certain parts of the world, but mostly in Asia and Africa. The nut of the Areca catechu palm tree has psychoactive and stimulant effects. I saw for the first-time people chewing betel nut (Maak) in Thailand (Buriram province). In Taiwan and Thailand people chewing betel nuts for 1000s of years. The archaeologist excavated human teeth containing trace elements of betel nut, dating back 4000 years. Chewing betel nut was always been an important part of Thai culture. Traditional chewing in the Thai way (Chian Maak) needs three main ingredients: Betelnut, Betel leaf, and red limestone paste. Betel Leaf is known as Bai Plu in Thailand. You will see many Grannies "Yai's" in Isaan province with black teeth. Except for the increased risk of oral cancer, some studies showed that chewing betel nuts regularly can be bad for your blood pressure, heart rate, and asthma.

Betel nut consumption has been also linked to the incidence of metabolic syndrome. In my opinion, moderate consumption is the key to the health benefits of this nut.

Durian:

It is referred to as the "king of fruits," therefore in a sense, it qualifies as a superfood or, more accurately, a superfruit. This fruit has many haters (because of the strong smell) but also many fans. It is native to Malaysia, Brunei, Singapore, Thailand, and Indonesia. This fruit is well-known to me. Around April is Durian season, and you will see many Thai people standing in long lines to get this expensive fruit at a discounted price.

Durian Nutrition Facts: It contains vitamin C, thiamin, niacin, folic acid, riboflavin, vitamin A and B6. Potassium, calcium iron, zinc, magnesium, phosphorus, sodium, and nutrients such as phytonutrients, protein, water, and some healthy fats.

Durian and Alcohol: Because durian will give you some hotness, some will advise you to not drink alcohol after eating this exotic fruit. Actually, there is no evidence to show that alcohol and durian are a bad combination.

For sure it can sometimes cause bloating and general discomfort, especially if you have consumed excessive amounts.

Can Boost your Libido: Durian can raise your body temperature, and Southeast Asians believe this is due to its aphrodisiac properties. According to some researchers in India, this urban legend is real. In my opinion, this small effect on libido is because durian contains zinc and folic acid.

Reduces Blood Pressure: It's rich in potassium and when plenty of potassium is present, the blood vessels can relax and reduce the stress on the cardiovascular system.

It's Good for the Skin: Durian is rich in vitamin C more than any other tropical fruit. Vitamin C has antioxidant properties to reduces the appearance of pigmentation and wrinkles.

Increases Immunity: As I said before, it has a large amount of vitamin C and many other vitamins and minerals that are useful for keeping the immune system strong.

Durian can Help with Insomnia: Another great benefit of durian is that can really help people who suffer from insomnia, as it contains tryptophan, an organic chemical that can make you relax and help you fall asleep easier.

It's a Natural Anti-Depressant: Studies showed that low levels of serotonin can actually cause depression. This fruit can make you happy as it contains happy chemicals like the amino acid tryptophan which is converted to serotonin.

It's Good Source of Energy: Durian is one of the best snacks to eat before going to the gym, as it is high in carbohydrates, a small amount of protein and healthy fats.

Promotes Bone Health: It's rich in magnesium, iron, manganese copper, and potassium and all of them are good for bone strength and durability.

Butea Superba:

Superba is a herb that comes from South East Asia. I saw Butea Superba for the first time in Thailand. Locals used it as an aphrodisiac for many years. Studies have found that is one of the best herbs for men with low libido. Butea Superba has active compounds called cAMP phosphodiesterase inhibitor, that boosts testosterone.

Noni and Graviola:

Cancer-fighting fruits like Noni and Graviola are used a lot as medicine in Southeast Asian countries. Noni juice has anti-aging properties and is used to reduce bad cholesterol and triglyceride. Can treat many diseases like arthritis, diabetes, depression, hypertension, and irritable bowel syndrome.

It reduces chronic pain, boosts the immune system, and detoxifies the body. Finally, it prevents cancer as it has cancer-fighting nutrients.

Kopi Luwak:

Denpasar means the north market and is the capital of Bali. At the traditional Badung Market, you will find fresh exotic tropical fruits, vegetables, flowers, herbs, and spices. At Badung Market, you will find also the world-famous Kopi Luwak coffee. Kopi luwak is one of the most expensive coffees in the world due to its quality and health benefits. It is produced from coffee cherries that have been eaten, digested, and collected from the feces of the Asian Palm Civet.

Kopi Luwak is less bitter than normal coffee and has less acidity. This is happening because during the process digestive enzymes change the structure of proteins in the coffee. Kopi Luwak in my opinion has more antioxidants, is a bit smoother, less bitter, and extremely overpriced.

Mangrove Trees:

I went on a mangrove forest tour during my vacation to the Indonesian island of Bintan. Southeast Asia has the largest extent of mangroves on Earth. Botanists believe that mangroves originated in Southeast Asia. Mangroves are essential to maintaining water quality. Studies have shown that Mangroves have antiviral, antibacterial, and antifungal properties. The most important is the antibacterial activity against Antibiotic-resistant pathogenic bacteria. Also, it is used as medicine in cases of hematuria (presence of blood in the urine).

Thanaka:

At Yangon Farmers Market, local farmers sell everything, organic vegetables, fruits, eggs, honey, and of course Thanaka bark. Myanmar women have been using Thanaka for more than 2,000 years. Tanaka powder and paste are made from the bark, wood, or roots of the Thanaka Burmese tree and it's a distinctive feature of the Burmese culture. This root is known for its properties to make skin whitening and soft and can reduce blemish and dark spots! Many Thai celebrities use Tanaka-cosmetics all time. These trees grow slowly in central Myanmar's dry zone. Trees must be at least 35 years old to yield good-quality cuttings.

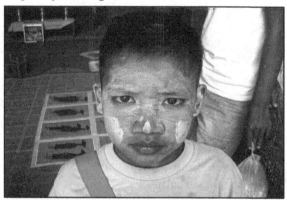

Women and girls have commonly applied this yellow-white cosmetic paste to the cheeks, noses, and foreheads! Thanaka tree has two active compounds, coumarin, and marmesin, you can use this root as a facial mask, face powder, and facial cleansing. This bark it's an ancient beauty secret with powerful skin benefits.

Thanaka is also used as a medicinal product to treat acne, skin sores, fungus, poisoning, measles, and even epilepsy and fever.

Southeast Asian Massage Therapies:

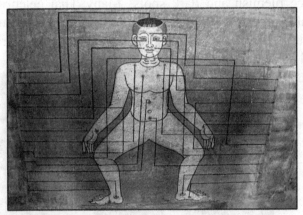

Without a doubt, Southeast Asia is the Mecca of massage treatments. You will find massage therapies in almost all Southeast Asia countries. Especially in Thailand, Laos, Cambodia, Vietnam, Indonesia, and the Philippines.

Thai Massage Treatment:

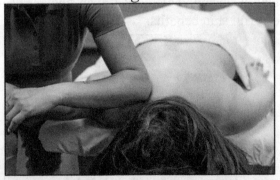

In Thai temples like Wat Pho, I discovered many ancient wall paintings that show the acupressure points according to Thai medicine. It is also called Thai yoga massage, as it has influences from Buddhism religion, traditional Chinese medicine, and Ayurveda medicine. Thai massage started 2500 years ago by Jivaka Kumar Bhaccha (Shivago Kompara) a healer and friend of Buddha. It's a traditional healing system combining acupressure, stretching, and pulling techniques to relieve tension and improve the flow of energy throughout your body. Thai foot massage is an offshoot of Thai Massage and the reflexology techniques originated by the Buddhist monks of the Thai Royal Palace. Thai traditional massage has many health benefits for the brain and body. In Thailand, the head it's considered a sacred part of the body and in some Thai massage places, they will ask your permission before touching your head. As Thai massage, it is known for its ability to clear the energy pathways is exactly what you need for overall well-being and rejuvenation.

Thai Blind Massage Institute:

Some people claim that the best massage techniques come from blind people. So, I said to give it a try and I went to TBMI (Thai Blind Massage Institute) in Pattaya. Blind people have been trained to massage and have "seeing hands". In my opinion, Thai blind massage is stronger and more intense. They told me that this is due to their heightened sense of touch. The massage was really good, and I was satisfied. Please note that the masseurs are not always completely blind.

Benefits of Traditional Thai Massage:

Eases Muscle & Joint Pain: Thai massage techniques alleviate tension in joints and muscles. *Providing an Energy Boost:* The techniques performed during a traditional Thai massage unblock certain areas and channels of the body and help blood flow and Sen energy. *Mental Health Care:* Thai massage offers a mindful rest and reduces stress. It releases nerve tension and can help the body and mind to relax. *Circulatory & Lymphatic System Boost:* As I mentioned before this massage promotes the circulation of blood in the entire body. The repeated slow and gradual acupressure techniques allow the lymphatic system to move toxins and waste out of the body.

Balinese Massage Treatment:

In Bali, you will find plenty and affordable spa resorts. From Kuta and Nusa Dua to Seminyak and Ubud. In these Spa-Hotels, you will find many experienced Massage Therapists. Balinese massage is an ancient healing therapy and a great alternative medical treatment. Is part of the traditional culture of Bali. Today it has been expanded to cater to tourists. It's a combination of various massage techniques. Compared to Thai, Balinese massage is not painful and there is not so much stretching.

Anyone can benefit from it, but Balinese massage can help with many disorders and diseases, including migraine, muscle, and joint pain, arthritis, allergies, sleep disorder, asthma, stress, anxiety, and depression. Normally, you will feel the benefits right after the massage therapy.

Achieve body wellness and unblock qi pathways with easy stretching, acupressure, aromatherapy, friction, and toning techniques. Be sure that the therapists you are a message with are well-trained otherwise you will get the opposite results.

Balinese Massage Benefits:

Improvement of blood and oxygen circulation. It balances the body. It boosts immunity levels. Relieves sleep disorders. Alleviating strained muscles and joint pain. Energizes the body and relieves body tension. It recharges the Human system. It relieves migraines.

Lao Massage Treatment:

Lao massage is similar to Thai massage but uses slightly different techniques. You can find massage shops in every little town in Laos, but you will find many of them in Vientiane. Like Thai massage, traditional Lao massage uses pressure points with rhythmic repetition. Some techniques are different, as I mentioned above. In Lao massage, the practitioners start with both legs instead of left to right leg like in Thai massage and move in your back. Lao massage is also a little lighter on stretching. There are three main massage types available in Lao: The Herbal steam massage, the oil massage, and the traditional Lao massage, which is the most common. *Prices*: The price for a traditional Lao massage usually is about 300 baht per hour in a normal massage shop.

Lao Herbal Steam Sauna and Massage: If you want something more traditional, visit the Lao Herbal Steam Sauna and Massage. It's a small traditional place in nature with basic facilities. The ladies in Lao Herbal Steam Sauna and Massage gave me an authentic Lao massage experience. The steam sauna is a must-visit, as you steam with a blend of fresh spices and herbs such as mint, lemongrass, and eucalyptus.

Top Places to Massage in Vientiane:

Pakpone Massage. Lotus de Lao Spa & Massage. L' Hibiscus Massage & Spa. Mandarina Spa and Massage. Herbal Steam Sauna and Massage. White Lotus. Massage and Beauty. Champa Spa. Chumpa Spa and Massage. Champakham Spa Lao-Mekong Massage. DA-O Massage. Lao Red Cross Massage and Sauna Center. Nirvana Spa Massage.

Hilot Massage Treatment:

Hilot is the traditional medicine of the Philippines. The knowledge and practice of Hilot are passed from generation to generation and have been practiced long before the Spaniards came to the Philippines. A Hilot therapist called Manghihilot, and focuses on bringing the five elements (Earth, Water, Air, Fire, and Spirit) of a patient into balance.

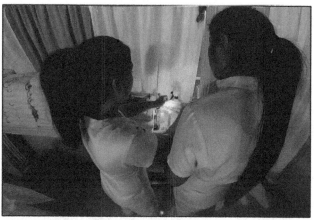

Although the original authentic Hilot therapy can be painful, this treatment is known for its therapeutic benefits. Warm strips of banana leaves are applied on the Back Body and pulled gently for cleansing, and detoxifying results. Banana leaves release oxygen and absorb carbon dioxide on the surface of the skin. In the end, the Hilot therapist performed deep strokes on the feet using tools called dagdagay sticks.

Hot Stones Massage Treatment:

The hot stone massage was practiced in Ancient Greece and Rome. Romans used the stones in Roman baths for healing purposes. The practice of hot stone therapy in Asia started in China 2,000 years ago and came to Southeast Asia much later. During a hot stone massage, volcanic heated stones retain heat and are applied to specific parts of your body for healing and relaxation.

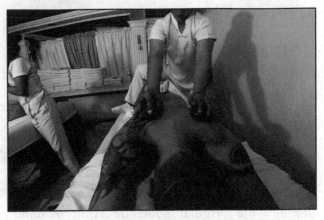

Hot Stone Health Benefits:

Relieves muscle pain and improves muscle relaxation. Reduces stress and anxiety. Improves blood circulation. Promotes sleep and increases flexibility.

Southeast Asian Martial Arts:

My first experience with martial arts started when I was 22 years old in Greece. Karate was more famous at that time. Shotokan Karate is one of the major sub-styles of Karate. This traditional Japanese martial art comes from the island of Okinawa and was developed by Master Gichin Funakoshi. Training in any martial art can do much more for you than just self-defense. When I was in China, I also practiced the 24 forms of Tai Chi martial art, but Southeast Asia has some of the most effective martial arts styles for self-defense in the world. The Indonesian Silat, the Khmer Bokator, the Burmese Bando, the Filipino Escrima, and of course the world-famous Muay Thai are some of them. Martial arts have many health benefits and can improve your overall well-being. As a big fan of martial arts, I couldn't resist practicing some of them. Today, I have some basic experience in the most effective Southeast Asian martial arts: Muay Thai, Filipino Boxing, and Kali-Arnis-Eskrima.

Muay Thai:

Muay Thai history starts in the 16th century when the Burmese army occupied Ayutthaya, the old capital city of Siam. For that reason, Muay Boran was secretly practiced by King Naresuan's soldiers. Muay Boran is considered the ancestor of modern-day Muay Thai and has many different techniques. Muay Thai uses the entire body as a weapon.

As Muay Thai uses not only the arms and legs but also shins, knees, and elbows is also called the "martial art of eight limbs". Muay Thai fighting style has many influences from other combat styles found in Southeast Asian minorities and tribes.

Thai Boxing Effectiveness:

Even before living in Thailand, I've always been fascinated by Muay Thai martial art in movies and real fights. So, I decided to learn some techniques of this ancient martial art. I practiced for two years and tried many schools in Pattaya. Is Muay Thai effective for self-defense? It is actually one of the most effective martial arts in the world. To someone with no fighting knowledge, Thai people look small and weak but believe me that's not the case when comes to a fight. From my experience, I can assure you that Muay Thai fighters are some of the stronger fighters out there and many steroid looking foreigners usually lose in the ring. Thai boxing involves full-body workouts and the deeper you get into your Muay Thai training the more you will realize that this martial art has numerous techniques and styles.

Muay Thai Clinch: Muay Thai clinch is one of the most important integral techniques of the sport and the reason why Thai boxing is more effective than kickboxing. The Muay clinch is stand-up wrestling with elbow and knee strikes. The fighters try to dominate to lock or throw down the opponent.

Muay Thai Health Benefits:
Thai Boxing has many health benefits, as it is training your body and mind. Many of the Muay Thai health benefits are the same as in other martial arts.

Strengthens Your Mind:
One of the biggest benefits of Muay Thai is that it changed my perception of goal setting and makes me look at any problem with courage. It boosts memory, focus, confidence, and keeps the brain young.

Improves Cardiorespiratory Endurance:
Most of the time Thai trainers will push you to your limits. Thai Boxing is aerobic and anaerobic it increases your stamina and promotes heart and lung health.

It's an Effective Martial Art for Self Defense:
As I mentioned before Muay Thai is one of the most effective Martial arts in the world.

Stress Relief:

According to experts, Martial arts allow you to release stress physically. Thai Boxing is the best medicine against emotional, physical, and mental stress.

Promotes Bone and Muscle Strength:

Combat sports can be a major factor in gaining muscle and bone mass. Muay Thai is an incredible workout and reduces the risk of osteoporosis and muscle atrophy.

Self-Discipline:

The ability to discipline yourself is a great benefit of martial arts. The Art of Eight Limbs is an excellent way to enhance self-discipline and self-control.

Professional Muay Thai Fighting:

Authentic Muay Thai fights can be seen at a variety of places throughout Thailand, but mainly in Bangkok and Pattaya. Watching fights in the city is a must for Muay Thai fans, but even for casual tourists, it is an experience not to be missed.

Tonight, one of my favorite trainers will fight in Pattaya MAX Muay Thai stadium, for the Championship finals.

Fighting in a professional fight is truly hard and needs a lot of preparation, but the rewards are well worth it!

Kali-Arnis-Eskrima:

Filipino Martial Arts were founded long before the Spanish arrived in 1521 and have numerous branches. Kali was taught at the various Filipino villages and until the early 900 was hidden from foreigners, or camouflaged as dance. These Martial Arts are so effective that has been adopted by International Special Forces Units. Filipino Martial Arts mostly use hard bamboo sticks, empty hands, and various bladed weapons. Arnis, Eskrima, and Kali combat styles influenced each other and all these martial arts belong to the FMA system. Kali is the oldest term, these martial arts were forbidden during the Spanish occupation and the use of sticks came as a sword alternative. Like the Israeli Krav Maga, Kali was designed to be a practical fighting technique. Bruce Lee also understood that Filipino Martial Arts are very practical and effective and integrated Kali into his Jeet Kune Do system. Somewhere on the rooftops of Manila I met my Filipino trainer and made some private lessons in single and Double stick training. I learned some basics and I improved my hand-eye coordination, speed, and control. Arnis teaches you discipline and control, is a full-body workout, and is great if you want to adapt in your MMA system to an effective weapon-based martial art.

Filipino Boxing:

The Philippines played an important role in Boxing history and evolution. I couldn't resist during my visit to Manila to

practice and learn some moves from the world-famous Filipino boxing. The sport of boxing was brought to the Philippines by the Americans and mixed up with the local Suntukan, also known as Mano-mano. Suntukan is the empty-hand section of Kali martial art and derives from the Tagalog word punch. If you are a fan of this sport then for sure you know many great Filipino fighters such as Pancho Villa, Speedy Dado, Manny Pacquiao, Nonito Donaire, Luisito Espinosa, Bobby Pacquiao, and so on. Boxing is one of the most popular combat sports and is one of the best backgrounds for MMA. It's great Self-defense, improves reflexes and body awareness, boosts your self-confidence, and you become mentally stronger. Boxing training is based on explosive strength training and technical exercises.

Each boxer develops their style, but one thing is for sure, you need to be mentally strong and have a good strategy.

Boxers think ahead like chess players. Today, I'm still practicing boxing and kickboxing at home together with other martial arts for wellness and wellbeing.

Southeast Asian Traditional Dances & Theatre for Wellbeing:

The theatre, music, and dancing in Southeast Asia have the same roots, Hinduism and Buddhism. Laos, Cambodia, Indonesia, and Thailand have similar musical instruments like metallophones. String instruments like the kecapi in Indonesia or khim in Laos, Thailand, and Cambodia is another example.

Health Benefits of Dancing:
Dancing has many physical and mental benefits. It's a good physical activity. It prevents falls and helps with balance and flexibility. Reduces pain and stiffness, improves your mood and social life. Reduces the symptoms of depression and anxiety. Dancing has impressive anti-aging benefits and it's a good activity for weight loss.

Thailand Traditional Dance:

Traditional Thai drama dancing like Khon is based on the classic Hindu Ramayana epics. Khon comes from the Ayutthaya Kingdom and is one of the six traditional Thai dance forms. Li-khe is another popular form of dance in Thailand. If you visit Thailand, you will notice that Thais are

great dancers. Thais appreciate life. The Buddhist traditions strongly influenced Thai culture. The word Sabai Sabai is usually translated as "happy". There's no literal translation to English, but its use is often meaning "to be well". The word Sanook in Thai means fun, but In Thailand, fun it's a way of life. Sanook is more than fun is wellness. Well-being is an important subject in Thai culture. Many people believe that the Indian Yoga mudras are simplified in many southeast Asian dances to a form of basic hand gestures. Hand Mudras help in conveying and expressing emotions during dancing.

Cambodian Traditional Dance:

During my trip to Phnom Penh, I visited many times the Royal University of Fine Arts. Apsara dance derived from Hindu mythology and was the classical dance for the royal court. This dance started at the time of Angkor and developed in the late 1940s. Deities, giants, and gods are dancing together in Cambodian Traditional Drama dances. The Royal University of Fine Arts trains folk dancers that depict aspects of Khmer life. The spiritual art of theatre and dancing is passed down from generation to generation. Khmer classical dance is the premier performing art and the symbol of Cambodian culture.

Balinese Traditional Dance:

In Bali, traditional activities and performances which are not influenced by western traditions have been a part of the island for generations. Ubud is one of the best places to see traditional Balinese dance dramas accompanied by superb traditional orchestras. The body movements in the sacred dances of Bali are symmetrical. Especially the eyes and feet are very important. The Eye movements are rapid and the toes are featured with raised and heightened positions. For more than a century Ubud has been the island's preeminent center for fine arts, dance, and music. Throughout the years, dance and drama play an important role in Balinese culture. A truly ecstatic theatrical performance that gives peace to the soul.

The Kecak Dance:

Visitors to Ubud usually end up at a temple dance. The Kecak dance or monkey dance has become a very popular show for tourists to Bali. The gamelan is not there. Rhythm is provided by a chanting 'monkey' chorus. The polyrhythmic sound of the chanting provides the name, Kecak. Taken from the Ramayana, it tells the story of Rama, who with the help of the monkey army, tries to rescue his wife from the hold of the evil King Rawana. The scary Barong lion creature doing battle against the forces of evil, taken from the Hindu epic Mahabharata.

Southeast Asian Spirituality:

Many travelers visit Southeast Asia for wellness and spirituality. Philosophy, meditation, mindfulness, self-awareness, and compassion are some of the practices that travelers come to learn here. The majority of the people in South Asia practice Hinduism and Buddhism.

Southeast Asian Amulets and Sacred Tattoos:

The sacred tattoos and magical amulets protect and remind the wearer of the Buddha's teachings. They also help to enhance luck in different aspects of life.

Southeast Asian amulets have many different meanings. Not all of these amulets are Buddhist or Hindu, there are also nature element symbols, Necromantic talismans, Animist charms and even crystals and gemstones.

Phra Pidta:

Phra Pidta in Thai means 'eye closing'. The amulet you see in the picture is an original Phra Pidta amulet! I have the luck to own this original Phra Pidta amulet! The meaning of closed eyes Buddha is to be indifferent to all external temper and emotions. Some experts believe that is a form of evolution through the transformation of the God of Fortune or Sangajayana. I believe that the meaning of the Phra Pidta amulet is blind luck. After all, even the fact that I had this closed-eyes Buddha amulet in my possession was by luck! It was the first day that I opened my shop in Thailand and we called a monk from the nearby temple (Wat) to bless the store and pray for good fortune. When the monk was finished, my partner's (Jimmy) ex-girlfriend requested the monk to give Jimmy an amulet for protection, (normally most of the monks carry some amulets but most of them are fake.) The monk replied, "Yes, I do have one." Then he looked at me and said, "I'll give it to you." "Thank you for the honor," I replied, and the monk smiled and walked away! After a year, I went to an amulet shop, where they informed me that my Phra Pidta amulet is genuine and costs around 50.000 Baht due to the gold inside. To be honest, I have no plans to sell it.

Phra Pidta Effect:

Thai people believe that carrying this type of amulet might balance internal emotions to be stable and to bring unexpected fortune and wealth!

Nine Face Buddha Amulet:

This is a very interesting amulet. During Lord Buddha's lifetime, nine rich merchants had taken refuge under Lord Buddha. These nine merchants supported buddha's mission of spreading the Dhamma (overcoming dissatisfaction or suffering)! The nine Faces Buddha amulet (Phra Kao Nah, MaHa Setthi Nava Goth) can be used to ward off bad luck from ourselves and can attract good luck and wealth! Setthi" means millionaire in Pali and "Nawagot" means nine times infinity. The strong power of the amulet depends on the action and reaction of both monk who blessed it and the amulet's owner.

Sak Yant Tattoos:

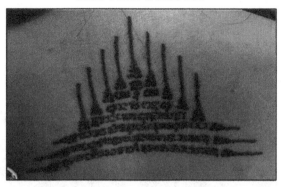

The magic Sak Yant tattoos are hand-etched (using a bamboo stick), ancient geometric designs mixed with Buddhist prayers. There are numerous sak yant tattoos that people get for a variety of reasons, but Gao Yord and hah taew are the most famous. Sak Yant Tattoos are believed to protect against evil and give powers for wellness, healing, strength, wealth and good luck.

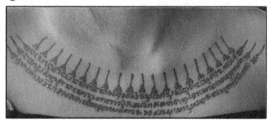

Many ancient cultures believed that the spirit is an exact copy of the human body. That coincides with the beliefs of many modern occultists about the astral body. The people of Borneo and especially the Kayan tribe, believe that their tattoos will help them to enter into the world of spirits. In many traditions, the practice of tattooing is a transmission of supernatural and magic between closed groups.

Some Thai people desire mystical abilities without having visible tattoos. They do an Invisible sak yant by using palm oil on the needle instead of dark ink.

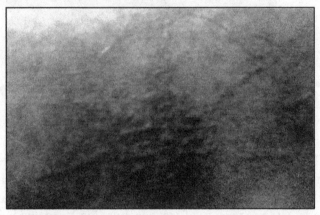

The discipline that follows a body that has received tattoos, reflects the concurrent subjectivization of the soul. If there's one lesson I took away from Thailand, it's to be cautious while experiment with supernatural forces. There are two types of Sak Yant tattoos: body designs and genuine Sak Yant tattoos. If you just want to get a Shak Yat tattoo then go ahead and visit any tattoo shop and just get it done, but if you want a genuine Sak Yant, tattooed by a Buddhist monk in order to attract wellness and luck then be ready for self-improvement too. Thais believe that in order to get a Sak Yantt Tattoo in a temple, you must be prepared to alter your lifestyle, or else the tattoo will turn against you. Originally, Buddhist monks carved Sak Yant into warriors seeking protection and strength in battle.

Yant or Yantra is any object used as an aid to meditation in tantric worship and Sak means Sacred geometrical design!

In this old photo, I'm getting a sacred Khmer bamboo stick tattoo during my first visit to Buriram. My ex-Thai girlfriend "Suttaoit" invited me there to see the second marriage of her parents, a custom of Khmer that exist for many years, so I followed her to Buriram.

<u>*Sak Yant Tattoos Meaning, Effects and Powers:*</u>
There are many styles of Yantra, such as Triangular Yant, Round Yant, Four Sided Yant, and even Pictorial ones.

Gao Yord: 9 Best Magical Spells, Master Yant.
Hah Taew: Represents the 5 yant or magical spells.
Round Yant: Represents Buddha's face.
Triangular Yant: Represents the Triple Gem of the Buddha Dharma and Sangha.
Four Sided Yant: Represents the Four Elements, (Earth, Water, Air, and Fire).
Pictorial Yant: (Animalistic) – Represents various Angels, People, and Mythical Animals.
Onk Pra: represents The Buddha Himself.

The Half Moon Symbol: Represents the Moon in the dark.

The Small Circle: (Sun Symbol) Represents the Sun and stars forces.

The Zig – Zag Spiral line: Represents the Saints who have attained the status of Enlightened beings.

Wat Bang Phra (Magic Sak Yant Tattoo Temple):

Wat Bang Phra means "Monastery of the Riverbank Buddha Image," This temple is a two-hour drive from Bangkok and is the most renowned temple in Thailand for making an original Sak Yant Tattoo! The exact year of its founding is unknown. The Wat Bang Phra Wai Khru, Tattoo festival is one of the most bizarre festivals worldwide. The temple became famous, thanks to Luang Phor Phern, a master in technical and magical sides of sak-yant. Another famous Sak Yant practicing monk in Thailand is Master Luang Pi Nunn. The recipe for the ink is secret and handed down from generation to generation, however, some claim it contains Chinese charcoal, sandalwood steeped in herbs, holy water, palm oil, snake venom, and even human remains!

Magicians, Healers and Theravada Saints:

As I lived in Thailand for such a long time, I experienced many unusual situations. Ninety percent of Thais hold supernatural beliefs. Ghosts, demons, and spirits play a big part in Thai culture and folklore. Ask any Thai whether or not he believes in ghosts, and he or she would look at you as if you have asked the most ridiculous question ever. Below are some unexplained stories that I witnessed.

The Holy Man of Buriram Province:

The first time that I came closer to Theravada Buddhism was during my visit to Buriram. My ex-Thai girlfriend was curious about the direction of our relationship, she, therefore, suggested that we visit one of the most well-known monks in the Isaan region. Together with other members of her family, we headed close to Surin in her uncle's truck. I asked her where we were going, and she said we were going to meet a holy man. After about an hour, we reached a temple close to a hill. The monk welcomed us while seated in the lotus pose. After a long chat with the family, He instructed some other monks to bring him the astrology book. After asking about our birthdays and reading his book, He began yelling at my girlfriend and looking at me with compassion. I was confused about what was happening, and when I subsequently inquired, my ex-girlfriend explained that he had been yelling at her because it would be her fault if we ever finished. Her account of the conversation with the holy man was undoubtedly incomplete. The monk was correct in his assessment of her, as she didn't be honest with me. This experience was intense and even though I wasn't very connected to Buddhism at that time, I immediately understood that this man was holy.

74

The Healer in White Clothes:

I saw this miracle with my own eyes. A Thai restaurant was located near my restaurant. The owner of this Thai restaurant had a very sick nephew. He seemed exhausted and had these flat red spots on his face that looked like measles. When I asked the girl who was cooking in my restaurant what was wrong, she responded that someone did Black Magic on him. Of course, I laughed at the answer, and I went back to work. After an hour, I noticed three Thai men entering the restaurant dressed in white. Everyone sounded serious, as they described the boy's condition. The head monk lit a ceremonial pipe and said some mysterious words, while the other two monks began to pray. Some friends (who were present) and I silently laughed at the situation. I continued with my work, and after 30 minutes, I saw the sick boy on a bicycle smiling without any spots. I was shocked, and I asked my cook again, "Hey, what the heck is going on here?" She then said, "I told you so."

The Monk of Yasothon:

This is a story that I did not witness, but I believe it because it came from a skeptical friend. Although I wasn't present, I trust this account because my friend doesn't believe in the paranormal. My friend and I first met in Pattaya, but after he fell in love with a local lady, he temporarily moved to Yasothon province (near Lao). He stayed at the home of his girlfriend, while the girl's family lived nearby. One day, she requested 1000 baht from him (about 30 Euros at that time). When my buddy questioned her about why she needed the money, she replied that she needs the money for her grandmother's treatment. The girl's grandmother was so ill that she couldn't even walk. The entire family packed into her brother's truck to transport her grandmother for treatment.

My friend asked, "Why are we going left when the hospital is located on the right?" "We are going to the temple, not the hospital", his girlfriend replied. My friend immediately thought that he had wasted 1000 baht for nothing. When they arrived at the temple, his lady advised him to go for a walk and to call him when the treatment was finished. My friend was walking around the temple and from a distance, he saw a monk blessing the grandma. Ten minutes later, his lady called him to return, and when he arrived, he witnessed the grandma walking and laughing as if she had never been ill. While he described this event to me in Pattaya, he looked honestly astonished.

The spirits of Buriram:

The month before I opened my restaurant, my ex and I were in Buriram. I asked her to perform Buddhist merit as I desired the business to succeed. When her mother knew about it, she asserted that she had a better solution. She gave us the directive to purchase a pork head at the market. I couldn't figure out what was going on. I assumed that we would go to the temple the following day. The next day six a clock in the morning, I woke up because of the prayers in the next room. The main room of the house was surrounded by elderly women from the village. My girlfriend advised me to eat breakfast before joining them. I sat with them and they started to pray in the Khmer language. After ten minutes of prayers, I suddenly experienced a shiver. When the old ladies had finished the ceremony, I asked my girlfriend's mum what was causing my shivering. She replied that some of the spirits that were present might have passed through me. I didn't like this idea, and I didn't ask for it. A traditional Buddhist merit was the only thing I desired. This was mostly an animistic ritual and not Buddhist. It is important in animist ceremonies to win the favor of the spirits that protect humans from other evil spirits by providing them food and shelter.

Theravada Buddhism:

Buddhism religion focuses on achieving Enlightenment through the Eightfold Path and the Four Noble Truths. Theravada, or "way of the elders," is the oldest of the three major Buddhist lineages and the one most closely related to the historical Buddha's teachings. It is the single surviving thread of the sects that formed after the Buddha's death. Theravada, also known as "Southern Buddhism". This religion spread across southern Asia, where it is still practiced today, including Sri Lanka, Myanmar (Burma), Thailand, Cambodia, Laos, and so on. Theravada is essentially a monastic tradition, emphasizing vows of sacrifice and self-purification, despite the Buddha's ethical recommendations. Theravada Buddhists aim to become Arhats (superhumans) in order to break away from the samsara cycle. According to Theravada, only monks can reach Nirvana, however according to Mahayana, both monks and laypeople can achieve Nirvana.

Theravada Meditation Techniques:

Theravada Buddhism concentrates on the eighth component of the Noble Eightfold Path, which leads to enlightenment similar to that which Buddha attained. This is the eighth and final section, which is all about meditation. The four foundations of mindfulness, as defined by the Buddha, are awareness of the body, awareness of feelings, awareness of mental processes, and awareness of truths.

In the Theravada tradition, there are two types of meditation: Samatha (calming meditation) and Vipassana (insight meditation).

Samatha - Mindfulness of Breathing Meditation:

The Thai Buddhist tradition is the source of the Samatha meditation technique. This Meditation helps to focus the mind and allows us to perform more efficiently in both our daily lives and our spiritual lives. Sit comfortably with your legs crossed, put your hands together and concentrate on your breathing, its natural rhythm, and flow, as well as how each inhale and exhale feel. Focus on the breath, and stop "daydreaming", now try to calm the "Monkey Mind".

Vipassana Meditation Technique:

Vipassana is a meditation technique that is used to gain insight into the true essence of things. Vipassana aims for long-term change. It is one of India's oldest, most traditional forms of meditation. The Pali word vipassana signifies insight into the actual nature of existence. Using this method, you practice self-observation by focusing on your inner self in a nonjudgmental manner. Sit comfortably with your legs crossed and put your hands in Gyan mudra. Close your eyes. Inhale deeply and concentrate on your abdomen. Do not attempt to regulate your respiration. Breathe slowly and deeply. Thoughts and imaginings are examples of mental phenomena and should be labeled. For example, if you have a mental image, label it "Mental image." If you're imagining hearing a sound label it "Imagined sound", and so on. You can train your mind to understand the true nature of mental phenomena simply by stating "mental image" or "imagined sound."

Best Temples in Thailand:

Temples are the best places for meditation. The Buddhist doctrine, the historic temples, and the country's emphasis on spiritual well-being were some of the reasons that inspired me to travel to Thailand for the first time. Because I lived there, I had the opportunity to visit some of Thailand's most famous temples. Here are some of them:

Prasat Hin Phimai:
The Prasat Hin Phimai in Nakhon Ratchasima:

Phra Pang Haan Yad:
The Phra Pang Haan Yad in Hua Hin:

Prasat Muang:
The Khmer Prasat Muang Singh in Kanchanaburi
Province:

Wat Pho:

The Wat Pho in Bangkok, also known as the Temple of the Reclining Buddha.

Wat Chalong:

The Wat Chalong, Phuket's largest and most popular temple.

Wat Phutthanimit:

The Wat Phuttha Nimit in Kalasin with the famous black Buddha.

Chiang Dao Cave Temple:

The Chiang Dao Cave Temple or Wat Tham Chiang Dao with the sleeping Buddha.

Wat Ku Kud:
The Wat Ku Kud, or The Chedi of Cham in Lamphun.

Phanom Rung:
The Khmer Phanom Rung temple in Buriram Province.

Prang Mafuang:
The Khmer Fruit-Shape Tower (Prang Mafuang) built-in Pre-Ayutthaya periods.

Golden Temple:
The Golden Temple in Bangkok.

Sukhothai Historical Park:

Sukhothai is one of the most important historical cities in Thailand. Founded in the 13th century and was the first kingdom of Siam 800 years ago.

The jungle literally swallowed up this magnificent city and kept it hidden for hundreds of years…

Sukhothai was a provincial town of the Khmer empire and it became the first capital of the united and independent Thailand.

Sukhothai temple ruins and the historical park is a
UNESCO World Heritage Site.

The word Sukhothai means Dawn of Happiness. The place
is full of historical relics such as ancient Buddha statues.

The temples and monuments of this ancient city have been
fortunately restored. Sukhothai historical park located about
12 kilometers from the new city and features over 190 ruins.
In the Old Sukhothai, I saw some of the most impressive
Buddha statues in Asia.

In Wat Chi Sum temple was an impressive 12-meter-high Buddha statue. The various styles of the temples are a result of Khmer, Sri Lankan, and Burmese influences.

Some of Sukhothai's sacred treasures were brought to Bangkok in the 18th century.

One of the best ways to see the ruins in old Sukhothai is by bicycle. These can be rented from a shop opposite the main park.

Wat Phapradoo:
Another great temple is the Wat Phapradoo with the left side sleeping golden Buddha in Rayong.

Tiger Temple:

The Tiger Temple was a Theravada Buddhist temple in Kanchanaburi Province. Unfortunately, the temple is closed to the public since 2016. About a year after my visit. Thai police removed the tigers, and the site was closed for animal abuse.

The Sanctuary of Truth:

Although not too old, it is one of the best temples I have ever visited. It is an amazing gigantic wooden construction and every square inch of the building it's covered with wooden carved sculpture.

I was really fascinated during my visit to the Sanctuary of Truth, as the temple manages to bring together a number of disparate beliefs of Southeast Asia.

Situated by the sea at Laem Ratchawet on Na Klua Road, North Pattaya.

The building has been under construction now for more than 25 years, and it might take another ten years before it is finished. Admission is 500 baht for adults and 250 baht for children.

Big Buddha Hill Temple (Wat Phra Yai)

It is the biggest Buddha image of Chonburi province and is visible from far away. Wat Phra Yai is near Pattaya City, located 2.5 Kilometers from South Pattaya.

The temple was established in 1977. The Buddha statue (Luang Phor Yhai) is more than 18 meters tall. Apart from the Big Buddha, there are seven smaller Buddha images on the temple grounds and a pavilion. There are about 100 steps leading up to the Buddha statue. The good news is that the entrance fee is free.

Tham Khao Luang:

Tham Khao Luang is located in Khao Luang, close to Phetchaburi City. This cave temple is a great spot for meditation, as it is full of Buddha images and footprints.

Wat Thaton:

Wat Thaton is located near the Mae Kok River in the village of Ban Thaton. It is an impressive temple with a large white Buddha image sitting in a meditation posture.

Wat Huay Mongkol:

Wat Huay Mongkol is located about 15 km from Hua Hin in the Ban Huay Khot area.

This temple complex is dedicated to the legendary monk Luang pu Tuad. The legend said that he performed miracles and that he is famous for his sacred protective amulets. Luang Pu Thuat was born in the southern Thai province of Songkhla in the year 2125 BE (1582 CE). Luang Pu's parents were poor Chinese farmers and were both devoted Buddhists. It's probable that they were overjoyed when their son began to show an interest in spirituality at a young age. He was well-known for his caring and generous nature. He never hurt other living creatures, whether they be

human or animal. Luang Pu had been demonstrating his miraculous powers since he was a small child when his mother went out into the yard one day and discovered an enormous snake wrapped around the hammock where her child was sleeping. No one could approach the hammock or the child because of the snake. After some thought, the parents concluded that the giant snake was an angelic Deity sent to demonstrate the virtue of their child. So, they ran out and purchased some puffed rice, flowers, and incense, then rushed back to pay devotion to the snake. When they finished making the offerings to the giant snake, it wriggled free of the hammock in which baby Poo was sleeping and walked away. With tremendous anxiety for the baby's safety, the family all raced over to the hammock cot. But, to their surprise, the infant was not only sleeping sweetly, but he also had a multicolored crystal on his chest that glowed with an unusual light. Luang Pu Thuat's family insisted on him receiving extensive religious education as he grew up. He began attending dharma classes at his local temple when he was five years old. The monks were astounded by how fast and thoroughly he absorbed his lectures. He had learned all of the lessons that the local monks could offer him within a few years, and he began traveling temples far away from his home to get extra training. One of the most well-known legends about Luang Pu Thuat is the boat trip to Ayuthaya that he took. The weather became increasingly harsh and the crew began to panic.

Luang calmed the waves and made fresh drinking water out of the seawater around the boat. Luang Pu Thuat had high expectations for what he could learn in Ayutthaya, which was the center of Thai Buddhism at the time. The King of Sri Lanka offered to give Thailand's leaders' boats full of gold if they were able to solve a certain Buddhist puzzle. All of Ayutthaya's senior monks failed at this job, but Luang Pu Thuat eventually solved it, cementing his monastic reputation. Luang became renowned for his psychic abilities, and many miracles are attributed to him. He died at the age of 120. Even after his death, he continued to assist his devotees. Monks at Wat Changhai began to have vivid dreams in which they encountered this spiritual teacher in other worlds. They were impelled to create pendants of him, which they discovered might bring the wearer good fortune and protection. These amulets are ideal for warding off evil spirits and demons, as well as providing protection from danger and ill influences. His pendants typically depict him in black, the black represents a mysterious atmosphere that surrounded him.

The statue of Luang pu Tuad in Hua Hin is 12 meters tall and sits on a pedestal with a wooden elephant on either side.

Ayutthaya Historical Park:

The city of Ayutthaya was the Thai capital for 417 years. Many ancient ruins and artworks can be found within the city which was found in 1350 by king U-Thong. The architecture of Ayutthaya is a fascinating mix of Khmer (ancient Cambodian style) and early Sukhothai styles. Ayutthaya was so splendid that the Burmese tried on several occasions to overthrow the city. Today it's the most visited historical park in the country. In the past, many Dutch, Portuguese, French, English, and Japanese Foreign visitors said that it was the most illustrious city they had ever set their eyes upon.

Wat Na Phra Meru Rachikaram:

This temple was created in 1505 and was the place where the king of Thailand and the king of Burma agreed for peace. It is a good example of a typical Ayutthaya-style temple.

Wat Yai Chai Mongkol

Wat Yai chai Mongkol, is located in the southeast and can be seen from a far distance. This monastery was built by King U-Thong, in 1357 AD. Especially for the monks who had returned from Ceylon.

Wat Chaiwatthanaram:

One of the most imposing Buddhism monasteries. Was established by King Prasatthong in 1630. It is believed that the temple is located on the site of his residence. He built this temple as a merit ceremony for his mother. The architecture is similar to that of Angkor Wat.

Wat Mahathat:

Also known as the Monastery of the Great Relics, it was an elite monastery. Wat Mahathat was once the seat of the Sangaraja, the leader Monk of the Kamavasi sect.

Wat Phra Sri Sanpet:

The royal palace was located here from the establishment of Ayutthaya. Later, king Borommatrallokonat built a temple on this site in 1448 AD to use it as a monastic area.

Wat Phanan Choeng:

Wat Panan Choeng is an old temple that houses a large golden Buddha statue of Luang Pho Tho. It's a historical statue and the symbol of Ayutthaya city.

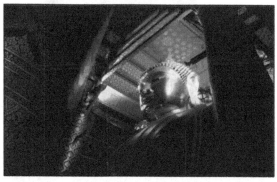

Wat Phra Yai:

The temple Wat Phra Yai is located on Bang Ruk village in the northeastern tip of Ko Samui.

Was built as a place to pay respect to the Lord Buddha in 1972, by the People of Koh Samui.

The giant 15-meter-tall golden Buddha statue of this temple is a major landmark of Samui. Most people that visit the temple admire the size and beauty of this remarkable statue. If you climb the stairs up to the viewing platform it offers superb vistas of the northern coast of Koh Samui.

On the temple, there are also warriors and gods from the Hindu and Buddhist religions.

Laos Vientiane Wat Xieng Khuan:

26 km far from the center of Vientiane, 30 minutes by car is the famous Xieng Khuan or like most people know it Buddha Park. This Hindu-Buddhist Park is one of the most spiritual sites I have ever visited. There are more than 200 statues (Shiva, Vishnu, animals, humans, and demons) filled with cryptic symbols! In my opinion, it's one of the best places to visit in Vientiane. The place is full of positive energy and mysticism. The temple was built in 1958 by the Luang Pu Bunleua Sulilat, a mystic-shaman yogi monk. After years Luang Pu moved to Thailand and created a similar park named Sala Keoku in Nong Khai. His sculpture-art is a mix of Buddhism and Hindu philosophy and mythology. The legend says that he was walking into the mountains when he felt near a cave the power of Rishi. He stayed inside the cave and meditated for years.

The statue in the picture represents the earth, the underworld, and heaven. The statue's mouth and entrance on the ground floor symbolize the underworld, the first floor the earth, and the roof represents heaven.

Inside Buddha Park, there are numerous sculptures of Buddha and characters of Hindu lore as well as many mythical creatures. Wat Xieng Khouang is not only worth a visit but your journey to Laos will be incomplete without it.

Malaysia Penang - The Temple of Supreme Bliss:

Kek Lok Si is the largest Buddhist temple in Malaysia. This Buddha temple was built at the end of a hill, near the village Air Itam. It is one of the best places to see on Penang and one of the finest Buddhist temples in Southeast Asia. Since the temple is close to nature and contains a large number of Buddhist scriptures it's a perfect spot and retreat for meditation and knowledge. The Buddha texts and the Monks at the Kek Lok Si temple can greatly assist you in your philosophical journey. Inside the temple, you will find many Vegetarian restaurants. The temple was begun in 1890 and completed in 1905. Kek Lok Si includes a lot of pagodas and other small temples. It is influenced heavily by Burmese, Chinese, and Thai  culture and art. There is also a gigantic statue of Kouan Yin, the Goddess of Mercy of Mahayana Buddhism. Kek Lok Si is also known as Ban Po Thar (the Ten Thousand Buddhas Pagoda). It's designed to symbolize the harmonious relationship between the Mahayana and Theravada Buddhism. The Supreme bliss Temple is popular among Taoist monks that trying to achieve immortality. There is also a wall, the wall of destiny and the monks stick to the wall, the wishes from the faithful people. A library with a large collection of literature on Buddhist philosophy is located close to the wall.

Myanmar Top Temples and Monasteries:

In Myanmar, there is a strong presence of the Buddhist religion and the Buddha's teachings. If you want to explore all of Myanmar's spectacular religious temples, stupas, monasteries, and pagodas, you will need to remain for years.

Sule Pagoda - Yangon:

Sule Pagoda is located in the center of Rangoon. This golden dome is 48 meters high and surrounded by astrologers and palmists' small shops. It is also called Kyaik Athok. It's built, in the typical Burmese Mon style with four entrances. It is said to be over 2,000 years.

Shwedagon Pagoda - Yangon:

Shwedagon, the mother of all Pagodas in Myanmar, is the landmark of Rangoon and dominates the shape of the city. Shwedagon means the golden pagoda. Towering to a height  of 326 feet on Theingottara Hill. The base is surrounded by 64 small pagodas. It is believed to have been built nearly 2600 years ago, that is, during the Buddha's lifetime. According to the legend, Tappussa and Ballika, two Burmese merchants that traveled around the world led a caravan of bullock carts to India and there they came across the Buddha who had just come out of seven weeks of meditation and recently attained His Enlightenment. He was sitting under a tree feeling the need for food. The two brothers offered honey balls to Buddha and received in return eight strands of the latter's hair.

The two brothers returned from their journey and enshrined the three hairs in a stupa where the great Shwedagon Pagoda is now built. It is believed in Myanmar that the hill upon which the Shwedagon Pagoda stands was not haphazardly chosen by

Tappussa and Ballika but in fact, is the site where the three Buddhas preceding the Buddha Gotama in this world, deposited relics.

Buddha Kakusandha left his walking staff, Buddha Konagamana left his water filter and Buddha Kassapa a part of his robe. For that reason, Buddha Gotama requested Tappussa and Ballika to enshrine his relics in this location.

Shwenandaw Monastery - Mandalay:

It's one of the most important historical buildings of Mandalay. It is famous for its wood carvings and it is a replica of the old Mandalay Palace. Originally was built inside Mandalay Palace, but in 1880 King Thibaw move it out of the

Palace and turned it into a monastery. This monastery is a masterpiece and a perfect example of 19th-century Burmese teak architecture.

Mahamuni Paya - Mandalay:

Mahamuni Paya is the holiest temple of Mandalay and it is regularly visited by devout Buddhists throughout Myanmar. Was built in 1784 and almost fully rebuilt after a fire in 1884. The famous Mahamuni Buddha is a huge 4m tall old bronze image blessed by Buddha Gautama. Rakhine kings believed that provided supernatural protection for their successive Kingdoms.

Here, you see the devotees, applying gifts of gold leaf on the body of the Buddha image. In this pagoda, the women are not allowed to touch the Buddha and have to sit in a separate place.

Shweyattaw Buddha - Mandalay:

Mandalay Hill is the landmark of the city. The Shweyattaw Buddha image is located approximately halfway up to Hill. It's a large golden standing statue of the Buddha commissioned by King Mindon. According to the legend, Buddha visited the top of the Hill he stretched out his hand to the plain below and prophesied that a great city and a religious center would be founded at its base. Mandalay Hill is 236 meters high and situated just northeast of the city. On top of the hill, you see a magnificent view of the city and surrounding countryside. On the top, you see also the Su Taung Pyi pagoda which was built by the great builder of Bagan, King Anawratha, in 1052.

Bagan Temples:

Bagan was the capital of Ancient Myanmar and today is the main tourist destination of the country. Nyaung, is a modern market town and an administrative center. It's the favorite home base for travelers who visit Bagan. Located 15 minutes from Airport and situated on the eastern bank of the Ayeyarwaddy River, about 193 km south of Mandalay.

Bagan was founded in 849 A.D. by King Pyinbya. King Anawrahta introduced Theravada Buddhism into Myanmar and Bagan became one of the most important centers of Buddhist learning.

Bagan temples are very similar to the temples of Angkor Wat in Cambodia. In Angkor, there are less than 50 monuments, at Bagan are more than 2,000 temples and even after the earthquake most of them are still standing.

Ananda Temple:

Ananda temple is one of the most famous temples in Bagan and one of the four main temples remaining. Located just to the east of the old city walls. King Kyanzittha was inspired by some Indian monks and their story of the legendary Nanadamula cave in the Himalayas.

Thatbyinnyu Temple:

Built by King Alaungsithu in the middle of the 12th century. Located just inside the southeastern corner of the old city wall, Thatbyinnyu is one of Bagan's tallest temples.

Mahabodhi Temple:

Mahabodhi Temple built by King Zeyatheinkha as a copy of the Indian Mahabodhi Temple in Bihar. There is a big sitting Buddha image at the lower level.

Bupaya Pagoda:

Known to be the earliest pagoda in Bagan. It's a small stupa situated on the bank of the Ayeyarwaddy River. According to tradition, is built by King Pyusawhti.

Nat Taung Kyaung:

Nat Taung Kyaung is a very old decaying wooden structure and located in the vicinity of Taung-bi village. This old and finest wooden monastery stands in a center of a wide variety of trees and vegetation.

Gawdawpalin Temple:

Gawdawpalin Temple is one of the most imposing temples of Bagan! Built by King Narapatisithu. Located north of the present Archaeological Museum. It's surrounded by 4 Buddha images on the four sides of the ground floor.

Thatmynnyut Temple:

Thatmynnyut Temple was built by Alaungsithu around the mid-12th century. It's the highest temple in Bagan (200 feet). Travelers coming here to watch the Bagan sunset.

Iza Gawna pagoda:

Iza Gawna is a two-story Hindu architecture-style Pagoda. This temple area is one of the less-visited places in Bagan, but in my opinion, it's worth a visit. Inside the temple, you can see a charming seated Buddha that touches the earth.

Bagan is the site with the densest concentration of Buddhist temples in the world. For me, the 2200 temples and pagodas which are surrounding Bagan was one of the best travel experiences I ever had.

Angkor Wat Temples in Cambodia:

From Sihanoukville to Phnom Penh and later from Phnom Penh to Siem Reap. On the way, I changed a car, a minibus, and a boat. Finally, I found myself on a truck that was full of baggage, and chickens and for my company, I had two Cambodians that couldn't speak English at all. Siem Reap is located 340 kilometers far from Phnom Penh. We stopped three times on the way for food and after 12 hours I was finally at my destination. Bagan, Ayutthaya, and Angkor wat temples were the top Buddhist centers in Southeast Asia. Angkor is one of the most mysterious historical places on earth. Although Angkor was never truly lost, the ancient Khmer empire was long forgotten by the Cambodian people. The country that today is called Cambodia is only a small piece of the great Khmer empire. From the start of the 13 century Khmers had complete control over the biggest part of Indochina. From the time of Javararman the second until the middle of the 15 century the empire was famous with the name kingdom of Camboujia or kingdom of Funan. France's rulers were the first Westerners that explored Angkor. Legends and stories were told about lost temples with Gods and Giants.

After years a France minority brought to light the lost city of Angkor in 1819. Restoration initiatives were initiated by French naturalist and adventurer Henri Mouhot. Today everybody knows that Angkor was the capital of the Khmer empire. These restorations ended in 1968 when the war in Vietnam begins.

The Hindu and Chinese influences are intense in Cambodia and this is why Angkor wat has similarities with temples found in north India and Nepal. Today archaeologists from all over the world protect and restore Angkor, as many secrets of Khmer history still missing. The kingdom of Funan was a Hindu kingdom. Without a doubt, the early Khmer kings worshipped Hindu Gods and many of the temples were dedicated to different Hindu divinities. The first Buddha statues in Angkor wat were built in the time of King Kaundinya Jayavarman as Mahayana Buddhism marked a radical change.

The transition from the Hindu religion to Buddhism was gradual. Theravada started in Southern India and Sri Lanka and the teachings spread across Southeast Asia. Today as previously stated is the main religion in countries like Myanmar, Thailand, Cambodia, and Laos. Theravada in Southeast Asia interacted with local traditions like animism, especially in Cambodia. Scholars often comment on the relationship between doctrinal Theravada Buddhism and animist practices. Beliefs in local superstitions like spirits, ghosts, etc. fully continued.

My tour in Angkor finished with the best way, on the top of the hills you can watch one of the most beautiful sunsets in the world. For me, the trip to Cambodia was a trip back in time. A journey through one of Asia's most powerful empires.

Balinese Hinduism and Besakih Mother Temple:

Balinese people live in harmony with nature and have strong spiritual roots, the biggest evidence after all it's the many temples and shrines in every corner of Bali.

Balinese Hinduism:

Balinese Hinduism is based on Vedic philosophies and writings. Hinduism is what makes Bali different from the rest of Indonesia. More than 90% of Balinese are Hindu, you can see Hindu ceremonies and rituals all around the island.

Hinduism in Bali has some influence from Buddhism together with Animistic beliefs. The main difference with Hinduism in India is that even if Balinese Hindus worship a lot of gods and demons, they believe in only one God, with the name Acintya or Sang Hyang Widi. However, in India Hindus are polytheists.

The temples in Bali are similar to the Indian temples and the ceremonies are based on spiritual Vedic practices and chanting of mantras.

Pura Besakih Mother Temple:

Pura Besakih Temple known also as the Mother Temple is the biggest and most important Hindu temple in Bali. It's over a thousand years old and located on the slopes of Mount Agung. You are not allowed to go inside the temple without a sarong. Besakih is the only sanctuary where a Hindu of any caste can worship. It houses the ancestral shrines of all Balinese Hindus. It's best to visit this temple at festivals and events, but it's stunning whenever you go there. At the top of the temple, you can enjoy the beautiful view. It's a massive temple complex with 23 separate temples, and each temple has its name, but the word Besakih as a temple refers to the whole temple complex in the area. The three main temples are dedicated to Shiva, Brahma, and Vishnu. The most important temple in the area is the Pura Agung Penataran. Mother Temple is a very important temple for Balinese Hinduism. For me, is one of the finest and most beautiful temples in Southeast Asia.

Cao Dai Temple in Vietnam:

Ho Chi Minh City is the heart of Vietnam and is still called Saigon by almost everyone who lives there. I decided to leave the center and travel 50 miles northern westwards of Saigon in Tay Ninh province to explore one of the strangest religions in the world. The story of Cao Dai starts in 1919, when Ngo Van Chieu, a civil servant of the France colony receives a message from a superior spirit. While he was resting, a huge shining eye appeared in front of Chieu. The eye is surrounded by a halo. The spirit told him to concentrate on the DAO, which means the way. In the middle of 1921, the spirit returns and gives a name to this religious concept, the name is Cao Dai. The difference  with other religions is that Cao Dai was not founded by a man, but instead, a divine message found the right person to spread the knowledge.

The All-Seeing Eye is found everywhere in the Cao Dai temple. Caodaism was recognized officially from the France colony in 1926 and undertake all the religions of Vietnam down from one eternal higher consciousness.

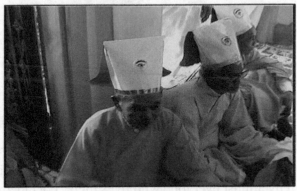

Starting with the most popular, Buddhism, Taoism, and Confucianism, and later with Christianity and Islam. The way and the beliefs of the Cao Dai religion were followed by many people including the famous writer, Victor Hugo. The basic theory of Cao Dai is that all the religions in this world have the same beginning and that all human beings are brothers and sisters under the same father the superior spirit. I was fascinated at the start with this idea as it makes sense. There is one God after all and we are all God's children. But as this religious idea sounds promising it's also hiding

a lot of dangers like the similarities with the New Order and the promotion of globalization. I'm still very skeptical about Caodaism Beliefs. Is this religion the cure for spiritual Greed or a deception?

My journeys in Southeast Asia and my search for wellness led me to explore new philosophies and religions. I understood that all people no matter what they believe have the same ethics and values. For me, this quest helped a lot with my spiritual growth and awareness.

Southeast Asia's Best Beaches and Islands:

In Ancient Greece, Thalassotherapy and Heliotherapy were considered a panacea. Southeast Asia has many exotic islands and is famous for its tropical paradise beaches. I believe that crystal clear water exotic beaches are ideal for wellbeing.

As I traveled to many countries in Southeast Asia, I had the opportunity to visit some of Southeastasia's best beaches and islands. Here is a list of the top beaches and islands in Southeast Asia that I have visited.

Koh Chang Island Beaches:

Koh Chang is the second-largest island, after Phuket, and the largest among the 52 islands of Trat. Its pristine white sand beaches are perfect for swimming and sunbathing. Some of the best beaches in Koh Chang are: Chang Noi beach, White Sand Beach, Pearl Beach, Klong Prao Beach, and Lonely Beach.

Phuket Island Beaches:

Phuket is approximately the size of Singapore and contains some of Thailand's most popular beaches. such as Freedom Beach, Kata Beach, Rawai Beach, Karon Beach, Nai Harn Beach, Bang Tao Beach, and the well-known Patong Beach.

Koh Samui Beaches:

Koh Samui means the island of coconut trees. This tropical destination has many beautiful fine sand beaches. Some of the best beaches in Koh Samui are Silver beach, Choeng Mon beach, Maenam beach, Lamai beach, and the most popular, the Chaweng Beach.

Ko Pha Ngan Beaches:

Koh Phangan is one of Thailand's true tropical gems and is well known for its Full moon parties.

The island is blessed with golden beaches like Haad Yuan beach, Haad Son beach, Haad Salad beach, Mae Haad beach, Malibu Beach, and Haad Rin beach.

Koh Tao Beaches:

It is also called Turtle Island and is often described as 'heaven under the sea'. Koh Tao's main attractions are snorkeling and scuba diving. Sairee Beach, Ao Tanot Bay, Shark Bay, and Sai Nuan Beach are some of the top beaches in Koh Tao.

Vietnam Halong Bay:

Halong bay is a nature miracle and one of the best places to swim in Vietnam. Located in the Gulf of Tonking and surrounded by 1,969 islands and islets. Ha Long means descending dragon and the name comes from a Vietnamese legend about a Mother Dragon. Ha Long Bay is the most breathtaking landscape in Vietnam and one of the best places to chill out in Southeast Asia.

Cambodia Sihanoukville Beaches:

Sihanoukville is Cambodia's fourth-largest city and Cambodia's major coastal tourist resort. The beaches, which are about a mile from the town center are beautiful with crystal clear aquamarine waters. Serendipity Beach, Occheteal beach, Victory

beach, Ream beach, and Sokha beach are some of the best beaches in Sihanoukville.

Malaysia Penang Island Beaches:

The beaches in Penang are bigger and wider. The best beaches in Penang are Tanjung Bungah beach, Pulau Jerejak beach, Monkey beach, Moonlight Bay, and the Gertak Sanggul beach.

Bali Island Beaches:

Bali is an eminent tourist destination in South Pacific. It's a beautiful island that is in harmony with nature, with amazing beaches and lush forests. Kuta is one of Bali's most popular beaches. Although currents make it less suitable for swimming, it's a very popular beach for surfing and a great surf spot for beginners. Kuta Beach is the place where you will meet surfers from all over the world. Surfing provides many health benefits. It lowers your blood pressure & decreases your risk of heart attacks. It is an excellent total body workout. Surfing brings us closer to nature. It boosts the immune system and is great for weight loss. Other great beaches in Bali are Jimbaran beach, Balangan beach, Sanur beach, Balian beach, Jimbaran beach, and Nusa Dua.

Bintan Island Beaches:

Under an hour from Singapore, Bintan Island is an island

in the Riau archipelago in Indonesia, located 10 kilometers east of Batam Island and 105 kilometers off the coast of the mainland. It's one of the most exotic islands I ever visited and a great choice for beach lovers. You'll be surrounded by magnificent white sand beaches, exotic jungles, and wildlife once you get on the island. Some of the best beaches in Bintan are Trikora Beach, Lagoi Bay Beach Hamid Beach, Sekera Beach, and the White Sands Island.

Boracay Island Beaches:

Boracay is world-famous for its attractive sandy beaches with crystal clear waters. White Beach, Yapak Beach, Diniwid Beach, and Bulabog beach are some of the best beaches on Boracay island.

The Best Natural Hot Springs in Thailand:

Hot springs have been utilized for healing for thousands of years. Mineral hot springs have been acknowledged for their amazing medicinal properties by societies for hundreds of years. Southeast Asia has many natural hot springs. I visited the Air Banjar hot spring in Bali, but the best natural hot springs that I have visited in Southeast Asia were in Thailand.

San Kamphaeng Hot Springs:

I visited the San Kamphaeng Hot Springs for the first time in 2001 and since then many things have changed. Today there are two mineral bath pools where you can sit and soak your feet or even take a bath. Located on the way from Chiang Mai to  Chiang Rai. At the San Kamphaeng springs you will find local sellers, selling eggs for those who want to boil the eggs into the hot springs.

Tha Pai Hot Spring:

Pai is located in Mae Hong Son Province, in Northern Thailand, and is blessed with many therapeutic thermal springs. One of the best Hot Springs in Pai is the Tha Pai Hot Spring. Located eight kilometers south of Pai. This hot spring is surrounded by nature. There are several pools with different heat levels, and the hottest pool has a temperature of 80 degrees Celsius.

Sai Ngam Hot Spring:

Sai Ngam is located about 15 kilometers north of Pai and is a relaxing place to hang out with beautiful crystal-clear waters. The surrounding area is a magical landscape where you can experience the natural beauty of Northern Thailand. The temperature in the pool is medium at 36-degrees Celsius.

Hindad Hot Spring:

The Hindad spring is one of the best hot springs I have ever visited in my life. Located 130 km. from Kanchanaburi province. These hot springs were accidentally discovered by the Japanese army during the construction of the "Death Railway" in the 1940s. Hin Dat is a natural spring and is set alongside a cool river. It has two geothermal pools with 45–55-degree Celsius water which is perfect for relaxing or even swimming. It is believed that Hindad hot Springs contain healing properties for the human skin and body. The water of this Spring has therapeutic benefits for many diseases, especially for beriberi disease and rheumatism. People can't stay in those natural pools for more than 30 minutes without a break. What makes these hot springs a perfect natural spa is that opposite the hot spring baths, is the cool river water! Once you've done with your bathing, traditional Thai massage is also available near the Hindad Hot Spring.

As I mentioned before Southeast Asia is one of the best destinations to visit for wellness and natural therapies. The spiritual practices and philosophies of Hinduism and Theravada Buddhism have influenced the food, martial arts, and way of living.

The wellness journey in Southeast Asia begins from the time you step your foot on this land and includes, meditation, relaxing spa treatments, and wellness therapies. If you have never been to these nations, I advise you to do so right away.

Please Consider Leaving a Review:

Writing a book takes a lot of time and effort. If you enjoyed this book and feel that you gained knowledge regarding your overall wellness, please consider leaving a review, just a line or two. I will appreciate it very much, as reviews are very important for independent authors like me.

Thank You.

77561233R00085